HOMO *TOO* SAPIENS

New Chapter Publisher

HOMO Too SAPIENS
A Consciousness Dilemma

ISBN 978-1-938842-44-3

Published by
        New Chapter Publisher
        32 South Osprey Ave.
        Suite 203
        Sarasota, FL 34236
        tel. 941-954-4690
        www.newchapterpublisher.com

Cover design by *Strixia.com*

Printed in the United States of Americ

**To Chris Angermann,
my challenging friend and editor**

ALSO BY PIERO RIVOLTA

Novels

Alex and the Color of the Wind
Sunset in Sarasota
The Castaway
Journey Beyond 2012
Bridge Through the Stars

Poetry

Just One Scent: The Rest Is God
Nothing Is Without Future
Going By Sea
One Life, Many Lives

New Chapter Publisher
Sarasota 2019

Contents

Foreword

Piero Rivolta has been called a Renaissance man, and rightfully so. An engineer by training, he built luxury and race cars during Italy's goldenage of car manufacture when IsoRivolta, the company his father founded, rivaled Ferrari, Lamborghini, and Maserati in design and originality.

He has bred horses and built motor yachts and large, ocean-worthy sailing vessels, helping design a hydraulic, retractable keel for shallow coastal waters. As a builder, he has developed residential communities and commercial real estate on several continents. A frequent patron of the arts, he created La Musica, an international chamber music festival in Sarasota, Florida.

In all these endeavors, Piero has sought both beauty and simplicity and pursued his unique vision. For him, form and function have always gone hand in hand. In other words, there is always a purpose to his creations that seeks to tell a larger human narrative while offering a sense of delight.

The same is true of his writing—both his poetry and prose. He means to share what he knows about life, not just to tell an entertaining story.

Piero manages to succeed more often than not because he is one of those rare individuals who combines a poet's passion for language with the specific observations and demands for precision of a mechanical engineer.

Of course, there is an overlap between the two enterprises. Poets are nothing if not precise: Only the exact, right word or image will do to convey what issues from the wellspring of their creative spirit.

Engineers have that quality, too—obsessive attention to detail. That is a good thing. Without it, a bridge constructed from the opposite shores will not meet as planned, but be off, if only by inches. Band-aids and duct tape are not reasonable solutions at that point.

Yes, there is something about Piero that is unique— an ability to observe and draw conclusions, both rationally and with romantic passion. Piero's poetry has metaphysical aspects and includes musings about God and immortality along with a deep, playful appreciation for the everyday pleasures of life. In his novels and prose poems—as he freely admits—the characters often become mouthpieces for his most cherished ideas, and his stories are designed to involve readers just enough so they will pay attention to what he has to say.

In that regard, Piero's writing is squarely within the romantic European tradition, which uses the novel as a vehicle to raise questions and make an argument about some aspect of reality. While many contemporary American readers may prefer emotional stories about relationships or genre fiction like sci-fi, mystery, or romance, Piero continues to set forth his ideas unapologetically.

Throughout his writing, he shares his discoveries about love and lovemaking, work, politics, government, bureaucracy, power, human desire, spirituality, freedom, history, religion, God and the mysteries of the universe. Big issues and questions, yes, and meant to provoke. Yet, approachable like the man himself, who does not put on airs. In the process, an attitude, a stance toward life emerges, a philosophy, if you will, although Piero would never claim to be a philosopher with a capital P. But he is a shrewd, perceptive, caring, even passionate observer of the ways of the world and the vagaries of the human condition.

This book, then, is a collection of his ideas, insights, observations and conclusions, disentangled from the characters he created to convey them. They are presented in the order in which the books were published. An earlier idea of grouping them by theme and category was rejected because it destroyed the discursive sense of discovery for Piero at the time when he wrote them.

As a result, there are some repetitions and overlap among the entries. But they also provide the opportunity to observe how his thinking has evolved, tempered in the cauldron of his life experiences, and what ideas have remained the same, like human bedrock—immutable, solid, part of our DNA.

I would suggest reading them like savoring a good wine—in small sips rather than hungry gulps. Let them swirl around in your mind a bit and then decide what to make of them and if they have the taste of truth.

Piero has always been a life-affirming writer, in line with his engineering sensibility—he wishes to solve problems rather than dwell on them, and to look back in time only in order to move forward.

The German poet, Rainer Maria Rilke, in his "Archaic Torso of Apollo," contemplates an ancient god whose image is broken yet continues to engage the viewer with an otherworldly force. He ends his sonnet with the unexpected line. "You must change your life!"

Piero's work challenges us in the same way to better understand ourselves—who we are, what we're made of, and what we are capable of as individuals and a species—and to act accordingly.

Chris Angermann
New Chapter Publisher
Sarasota, Florida, 2019

Preface

These collections of quotes, coming mostly from the characters in my books, are intended for those who appreciate my perceptions; notably, that simplicity is the mother of creativity and that curiosity is the daughter of intelligence.

The great human dilemma is that Homo sapiens, as a species, believes itself to be too wise and smart to waste time to focus on improving and evolving its conciseness and helping its ego to become part of the universe.

Thousands and thousands of years have passed amid practical and scientific discoveries that helped to simplify daily life and make it more interesting. But our lack of commitment to try to comprehend the role of our universal consciousness has resulted in a loss of usefulness of valid guidelines and friendly relations with the mysteries that surround us.

All too often, humanity gets caught in a fever of pettiness, as ''over-rational'' approaches and systems impose a myriad of rules and regulations to achieve political and religious correctness, generating fear, jealousy, envy and, ultimately, stress anger and disillusion.

In these periods of regression and darkness which, unfortunately, can last for a long time, all progress previously achieved is forgotten.

The cycle has to start again, but I can offer no conclusions: Such reality outmatches my abilities. I can only try to whisper questions to the elusive, vital consciousness, longing for a new renaissance....

Will I hear back?

Piero Rivolta
Sarasota, Florida, 2019

In a quiet morning, I had a close encounter with what is believed to be our consciousness, a reality deep within ourselves which seems to ignore time and place, but one that whispers.

I asked it if we, *Homo sapiens*, are wise species.

No answer.

HOMO *TOO* SAPIENS

A CONSCIOUSNESS DILEMMA

If you dare brush up to God, you
risk madness.

You'll scorch your fingers if you
dare touch eternity, burn your
eyes staring at infinity.

JUST ONE SCENT
THE REST IS GOD

Our culture is being smothered by people who talk at one another without communicating, media figures who overanalyze every event and decision, and lawyers and politicians who seem to believe that problems can be solved by passing more laws and rules whose overwrought language very few can understand.

. . .

We live in a time that overvalues rationality at the expense of intuition, sentiment and common sense. But to what end?

. . .

Too much reasoning is a dead end—you can just as easily prove that God exists as disprove it. Reason by itself does not settle anything. Nor has it any use for non-rational modes of perception, such as intuition, emotion and love. Yet what kind of world will we create for ourselves if we dismiss these qualities from our discourse and understanding?

How many words of love could there have been, how many talks about nothing, the only ones that reach the depths of man and stop time, giving us some hint of the eternal. An abstract concept, like infinity, that we have been stuck with, residue on our terrestrial skin from who knows what journey. Concepts estranged from the world we live in, unreal, immaterial, yet at the same time so alive in us that we shiver when we draw near. In their presence we sense the void, we grow dizzy when we try to touch them.

. . .

We can only guess what they may really be, barely brushing past them, defining them with signs and mathematical concepts.

. . .

When you get down to it, humanity has no desire to waste its time musing, loving.

Each race or social group must be able to recognize what sets it apart, what it loves and longs for. It must also admit that prejudice and social difference do indeed exist, that they are part of nature itself. It is up to us to recognize, mold and transform such profound differences in lifestyle into something positive and not destructive.

. . .

There is no one set of laws or civilization that is right for everyone. No group must seek to destroy those civilizations which benefit mankind.

At least once in each of our lives there comes a time when we experience sudden change. Something foreign, violent makes contact, or better yet, clashes with our most intimate sphere. We're faced with intense decision-making moments which we might superficially try to cope with, driven by sudden emotions and circumstances.

The absurd thing is that we'll never know if the decision made in such haste was right or altogether wrong. Any argument in favor of our choice could be refuted twenty years down the road. Our spirit will continue to swing like a pendulum for as long as we exist on this Earth—our life's great pendulum of doubt.

. . .

If we think we are truly sure of a choice we have made, it means we are nothing less than superficial, unable to envision alternatives. Either that or we are so dishonest with ourselves that we want nothing to do with alternatives. In reality, it's much more likely that we always nourish some doubt, at least in the hidden-most part of ourselves.

. . .

Certainty doesn't belong to the human condition yet is our greatest aspiration. Thus, through the papers we read, the television we watch, the information we get from the Internet, the sermons we hear, the environmental dogmatists we listen to, we are under the illusion that we have achieved a precise and detailed awareness of the mystery that surrounds us, called Life.

. . .

Lying at the basis of life, science, our discoveries, is always a postulate, an act of faith, a statement we accept as a given, on which we base our curiosity, our passion for dialogue. There's nothing rational about this initial act, it's merely intuitive, based on some initial vague idea.

It's like entering a dark room, and by the scent that fills the room it is clear that there must be a rose inside, but we can only imagine its color, its form; otherwise we can pass the time discussing likely possibilities. To cast away any shadow of doubt, all we need to do is turn on the light. But doubt is an integral part of the whole journey for all of us. We can only hope that after, we'll be given the chance to climb up a step on the ladder of knowledge, perhaps even reach the top.

. . .

In short, we must produce, eat, discover, squander, suffer, talk. In a word, we must live, live intensely so as to taste the coming of the day when we can turn on the light in the room.

Today success is measured more in terms of quantity than quality. And it seems that only repetitive and unrelenting marketing campaigns can succeed in reaching prodigious sales results.

. . .

With unabashed simplicity, I make my choice: My country will be the free world, my religion love, and my law the mutual respect of feelings.

. . .

I plan to write a book detailing my experiences, in the hope that somebody will get something out of it. For now, I can tell you this: There's not just one color of the wind. And its language may be interpreted in many ways. It reaches us from afar, brushes up against you and moves on. It's a kind of force that seeks to harmonize nature's elements—first by exciting them, mixing them up. Then, as before, it leaves them to battle it out among themselves.

It's hard to have a relationship with the wind. It's much easier to talk to the sea, the clouds, and even easier to talk to pelicans, seagulls, dolphins and all the rest.

The color of the wind is its secret.

ALEX and the
COLOR OF THE WIND

Walking along the beach induces you to reflect upon the experience of a lifetime, all concentrated in the few hours of one morning.

...

It's not the fog that hides thoughts, but humanity—in its desire that it be buried in the sand, where it is safe and strikes no fear in the world. The sand, though, is rife with creatures that dig holes of every shape and size. And no matter how microscopic those openings may be, thoughts manage to escape in tiny, haggard groups. Wet and chilled as they are, they feel weak and somewhat confused. Thus, it will take them quite a while to reorganize and find the strength to set off and circulate throughout the world.

Pleasures are beautiful and intense only when they carry within them the awareness of their own precariousness. Then, they slip away and you live in memories and the near certainty that you'll experience them again on day, at another time, in another place. Or perhaps you will experience these magical moments all at once—though you haven't the least idea where or when.

. . .

The thing that counts most in a building is proportion. The taste in the details may change, time may take its toll and erode, and sometimes soften, graceless and flawless particulars alike. What remains that impacts the lives of city dwellers over the years are forms and the relationships that unite them: simplicity, fluidity, harmony of volume, the clarity of the message that the building must convey—its functionality, and the balance between costs and manifestations of wealth linked to the particular use it is intended for.

Though its details are often not understood, this language influences the way passers-by perceive its impact.

. . .

Whatever the profession, the older one gets, the larger one's brush strokes can be.

. . .

The whole process seems backward—you have to acquire a great deal of knowledge in order to become messy. Only at that point, your messes will be rife with ideas, solutions, experience, simplicity.

. . .

In the past, one was allowed to improvise. It was okay to make mistakes as long as one strove to to do one's best.

An odd concept, it would seem—work as a means of distraction!

. . .

All it takes is adapting the concept of "having fun" to another type of use—apply it to work, and see existence transformed into a magical experience and receive pleasure from one's daily commitments.

. . .

Living has become difficult, burdened with rules and rivalries which spur the creation of even more absurd rules.

It is all justified by self-styled "great movements of thought" based on highly debatable principles, heralded by mediocre and shortsighted men who are gifted with a misguided cunning of the sort that proposes, "Let's slaughter the cow that provides the community with milk. I don't have to worry since I'm friends with my neighbor and he never lets me go without milk because he has his own cow."

. . .

The key to the entire "world system" is finding a conceptually simple solution. The incredible thing is that this always exists but it's so hard to see! It's so difficult that mankind will probably never have time to find all the possible solutions.

And that's why we thought up God. What a simple idea. To explain everything!

· · ·

An unstoppable impulse obliges us to create problems for ourselves and others at work, in our more intimate spheres, and even in the simplest forms of communication.

. . .

The worst damage a generation can do is to influence its heirs with so-called "surefire belief." In the end it's only weakness, an attempt to reassure or convince ourselves that such beliefs do actually work and are truly "safe."

. . .

It's better to let life run through you and distribute enthusiasm where it may, without crystallizing behavior and anointing with a sacrament something that is destined to change.

. . .

Everything winds down and reaches a dead point, stalls out. Then everything starts back up again, driven by the force of man's will and courage. It's a natural cycle, perhaps it occurs throughout the universe.

· · ·

Let the world turn without you—it's going to turn anyway. Let "your destiny" turn around you, undisturbed.

. . .

Experience, beliefs, culture—and entire patrimony accumulated—these are positive elements, but you also have to be ready to evolve, or stand by and watch. Why would anybody want to obstruct the course of evolution which, compared to the duration of human existence, seems to go round and round, endlessly reinventing itself?

Perhaps evolution is not he right term. It's just an ongoing perturbation, like the effect of wind on water.

. . .

The evolution of a people is slow; perhaps it is and will always remain a mere illusion. Positive cycles seem to be followed by periods of progressive destruction of goals attained.

. . .

It is necessary to evolve, even in the awareness that one risks returning to where one started from. This, too, is a change, perhaps a rediscovery, or even a recycling of ideas—but it is, in any case, evolution.

Change means life.

. . .

This is the air one breathes in America. It's an atmosphere in constant motion, where you're forced to seek out solutions. Details are worked out along the way.

. . .

How pleasant it is to relax aboard a plane after so much hurrying, pushing and shoving, waiting, taxi rides, goodbyes, questions, telephone calls, last-minute decisions.

You close the door on work, on your responsibilities, on having to pack your bags, on having to leave messages...the hum of the engines lulls you to sleep.

You're in someone else's hands, you might as well relax.... You cannot intervene. Just let destiny run its course.... whatever happens you'll wake up in another reality, a different city, with different customs, amid people who are different from the ones you left behind.... If worse comes to worst, you'll wake up in a completely different world.

. . .

A strange, cosmopolitan city like New York! It's like walking into a store in outer space and saying, "I'd like a sample of human activity on earth. A sample that explains a bit of everything like Reader's Digest. Later, I'll make a more in-depth study.

. . .

There is no other country where people are as passionate about politics as Italy. People there will discuss everyone and everything in politics at the drop of a hat, if only for the pleasure of complaining, boasting, offending someone, considering themselves better than anyone else on this planet, bemoaning their situation...and then everything goes on as before, unchanged.

. . .

For some strange reason, we feel responsible for the atrocities our ancestors committed as they imposed their way of living and thinking. What's more, we feel responsible for the mere fact that they even tried to impose their convictions, about whose intrinsic worth we ourselves harbor serious doubts.

· · ·

Writing about the past with the mentality of today, without making an effort to understand the reality and peculiarities of a different age, is almost a sacrilege. It's tantamount to wanting to create a third God to judge the other two, and to justify this act by saying our God is more democratic.

It's just that today it is lived and manipulated in a different manner.

. . .

Stress—is not that word the symbol of our times? We use it and abuse it to justify all sorts of behavior. And perhaps we get a certain kick out of using it. But is it really our invention, or have we but found a new name for one of humanity's old companions, weakness?

After all, stress is the same as weakness, which is the same as a flagging spirit, a lack of that fortitude which was so important back in the days of Republican Rome. Was fortitude the buzzword back then, the way stress is today?

We're running on a treadmill which remains stationary. The more we accelerate, the more we realize that the whole thing might come to a brusque stop any second. The faster the belt beneath our feet runs, the worse our fall is going to be if the machine suddenly breaks.

Perhaps the problem of stress is just this.

. . .

In life, an exciting situation that becomes drawn out for a lengthy period of time—no matter how pleasant it may be—puts a person's constancy to the test.

When peace reigns, people want to argue. When war ravages, they want peace. If the calm and excitement alternate, people become unaware of time passing, and as they age, they mutter away—but it is acceptable.

Even if we think good thoughts, the harmony of nature may break before our very eyes and blow us to extinction.

. . .

Sex doesn't necessarily have anything to do with beauty. Sex follows different paths for everyone, its ways are hard to assess and comprehend.

Some call it love, others sex, still others call it sin or betrayal. It would be much simpler to consider it for what it actually is—a mutual, innocent exchange of imagination and energy, something that reassures us that we are the product of the fusion of body and soul, which both require regular maintenance.

In truth, giving and receiving are separated by an almost imperceptible line, so fine we can barely make it out. For instance, it is commonly thought that a gift brings more pleasure to the person giving it than to the person on the receiving end. Indeed, the receiver may not even like the object that has been given to him or her, and what's more, must now devise some way of returning the favor. The giver, at any rate, is gratified by the act of giving.

. . .

There has to be a way to explain that helping your-self or someone else to be free is an act of love. Of course, this freedom must not hinder others' free-dom, nor should it offend to the point of no return the feelings and dignity of the other, which should go hand-in-hand with the right to be women and men.

. . .

If you want to enjoy the sunshine and take in the beauty of the flowers, you've got to put up with the presence of insects.

. . .

Drink your wine and get drunk on your thoughts. Our actions, our lives belong to us and only to us.

. . .

Deep down inside, almost all of us are just kids dressed as adults.

. . .

People were created to live together.

. . .

We just have to open our eyes and try to understand that behind any complicated situation lies a simple explanation. Perhaps too simple to be grasped, since for centuries we've been taught to reason according to very complex schemes. It is only by complicating simple things that people with no particular talent succeed in controlling the world. Let's take a minute and think it over. We may get lucky. Lightning may strike and ignite, within our minds, a flash of poetry, of creation.

. . .

My rights to freedom vanish at the beginning of the precise border with nature, with humankind. But nothing, not even a dream, is without future. Albeit grandiose and solitary today, my happiness is of the moment; it will not disappear completely as the years pass, as hopes begin to dwindle. It will slowly fade away, although something shall always remain, because nothing is without future, and when you live to love, you'll find that someone loves you.

NOTHING IS
WITHOUT FUTURE

If you think too intensely,
you stop laughing altogether.

You live
because life of
life is born
and no one knows
where the border of death lies.
Death may border on
a new life
and you must find love to find out.

SUNSET IN SARASOTA

What happens to our subconscious search for simplicity in life, that search in which there is an answer to every question?

. . .

Why do so many people create so many problems and take pleasure in fighting just to feel alive, indispensable, and thus important?

. . .

Some people say "No" only because they believe that if they don't, they'll be gripped by the fear that no one will realize they exist.

. . .

Life, however, is meant to be lived with actions and not merely in dreams and reminiscence.

. . .

You're only as old as you feel inside, as old as your spirit communicates to others.

. . .

Freedom is a difficult word to interpret and explain. It would be necessary to begin from the principle that freedom is more of a duty than a right. This is something that the world today tends to forget. In reality, however, this was to be expected, because you can't speed up certain types of evolution. The so-called cultural revolutions, which eventually break into all-out wars, lead only to temporary dominion. Things get back to normal in a short time thereafter. We progress, but we de fend the culture and the lifestyle that were fought so hard for.

. . .

Humanity seeks freedom, but people adore the rules that enchain them.

. . .

There have been lots of political parties, many governments, tons of ideas, and a host of divinities, but nowadays, there is only one terrestrial God that makes the world go round: money.

So at last, a common religion has been found, for which men argue and fight—seemingly, that is. When one faction wins and another faction loses, the equilibrium more or less remains the same, of interest to all.

. . .

The invention of money was a brilliant idea. Money is something so impersonal that, in truth, it means nothing. Can you eat money? Can you have fun looking at it? Touching it? Well, maybe someone who suffered from a bad case of greed and stinginess could!

. . .

If you don't use money, you'll soon realize that money itself is quite boring, and that you'll need to come up with another excuse for your life. Sure, that excuse might turn out to be something wonderful and good, but the danger is, it might also turn out to be something unhealthy for you and those around you.

. . .

Today we take it pretty much for granted that our security depends on having a home and money. The former represents a real need—perhaps that's why we call it real estate. We're not built to live naked in the wilderness. But in and of itself, is really quite useless. Imagine if the system were to suddenly change. For example, we conclude that aluminum is worth more than gold, and that money should be made out of ceramic and not paper.

. . .

Money represents but one aspect of the system, with all its defects and dangers.

. . .

One must live within the system, contribute to it, otherwise the system itself will crush you— either by taking away money you have earned, or by giving you more—so much money, in fact, that you risk merely admiring it. In the latter scenario, such sums may be useless if your life lacks passions, or even lethal because you have allowed the sense of their importance to grow within you, practically deceiving yourself into believing money is a living being with which to entertain a relationship.

. . .

Capitalism teaches how to use money to live each day as best as one can afford, not only to accumulate money or to use it to abuse others. (But that is a harsh reality.)

American capitalism is much more subtle: "I want to be happy and have the means, but I want others around me to be happy as well, even if their possibilities are limited, otherwise my life would become hell, an ongoing battle to maintain a standard of living and its relative pleasures."

. . .

Communism and socialism, on the other hand, have always achieved the opposite while preaching equality. The most extreme example is Russia, both during and after the fall of the Communist regime. Power and wealth concentrated in the hands of just a few violent characters.

. . .

The truth is that every system or civilization has a time limit that we tend to ignore, and we end up swimming in an unknown sea, thinking how wonderful the beach back there was.

. . .

How foolish to believe that a system can guarantee us all we need. It would be more honest to simply say, the system tries to do its best to assure you a happy future, but you, you must be the first to think of yourself and contribute to the well-being of the system through your commitment.

. . .

There are no first- or second-class jobs, whatever the job, as long as you do it well, as long as you're a consummate professional. Remember—if you want something special to happen, you've got to play an active role in society.

· · ·

One thing to understand—and this is the most important aspect of our existence—that nothing is guaranteed, and that we're on this Earth to give, not to receive.

· · ·

Thinking leads you to see how ridiculous the world is, even in its most profound misfortunes.

. . .

Men are born to live on the Earth. By nature, they have no desire to think. Indeed, they are born to live not to think. Those who think, who break life down in terms of pure thought may go far, it is true, but they take water for land and are doomed to drown.

. . .

Thinking too much can be fatal for men, as long as we walk the Earth.

. . .

Of course, intelligence begets curiosity.

. . .

Curiosity is the daughter of intelligence.

. . .

Kicking off an important conversation or discussion between two people who physically and mentally belong to opposite sexes is always a potentially explosive situation, a minefield that's best to cross cautiously for the safety of both.

. . .

You may eventually belong to the majority of the population that calls its partner either husband or wife, without truly understanding the complexity of the situation one has become entangled in. Such a relationship is important when it comes to raising children, but as far as other aspects go, it is purely a facade required by the legal and economic system.

Wouldn't it be better to call it simply an arrangement between two parties? Like all arrangements, it will leave room for possible modifications, since, as far as we know, nothing is definitive on this Earth. Perhaps not even death.

. . .

Many a time we seek out complete independence in our private life, yet so often find our spirit enveloped in a sort of solitude that, while it has its pleasant sides, may also harbor moments of profound boredom, which may even lead to states of dismay. Once we reach that point, a helter-skelter search for another person may ensue, someone with whom to share such moments, someone whose task it would be to brighten up our life.

. . .

Italy is a country that's truly enjoyable, if you don't take it too seriously. You have to watch out, though, and not get caught up in the system's pitfalls. You've got to measure your visits, as if you were taking a dive into its shimmering blue waters, then a swim and then out.

. . .

Many American women are attracted to Europe. At first glance, life there seems to follow a more interior path, there's something more human about it, and as far as Italy is concerned, more romantic. Everything appears simpler, more comprehensible and tolerant. Unfortunately, tourists are unaware that often, when passing from visitor status to actually becoming a resident, this view is shattered into tiny pieces.

Many do not lose heart, comforted by the fact that they possess an American passport and can return to the States whenever they want. For this reason, they don't realize that each day they stoop to new and strange compromises they never would have accepted in their home country—and they've slowly gotten accustomed to them.

. . .

Women are often quick to pick up on big changes, yet maintain a profound sense of reality in their attempt to bridle violent developments in themselves, and avoid sudden disasters. Men sometimes like to play the knight in shining armor who aggressively pursues, without a second thought, the ideas that have influenced them. An exception must surely be made for the so-called "fanatical" women, who are often intimidated by the male condition that they themselves secretly envy. These women are always ready to foment, with admirable determination, complications and useless friction.

. . .

Love for a god or gods, as in paganism; love for a person, for one's country, for one's house, one's land; the stars, the sea, etc., is the single force that our lives are led by. It is a legitimate force which must be cultivated in each of us without negative interference from the outside world. Love is ours, and it remains only for us and for those who share it with us. It requires no explanations, considerations, bonds or limits, because Love cannot distinguish them. Indeed, Love comes from nothing. If it is not accepted, it vanishes into nothingness.

. . .

Am I a person, a single, unique entity—someone who knows what he wants to do?

Does everybody feel this way?

Or is each of us a compilation of different personalities that sometimes think and act as one, and at other times are in contrast?

. . .

There is something inside of us that does not reason, something that lives a life apart, within its own confines and dreams of creation, whether or not such dreams come true.

. . .

I believe in the Universal Force. I believe that we are destined for more important things. I believe in something you can call God, or whatever you want to call it.

. . .

Christianity claims that we are all children of God, though this may be merely a metaphor to explain something more profound. Perhaps it means to tell us that we are a part of God, as a child inherits flesh and blood from his or her parents, as well as—to a certain degree—virtues and defects, bodily health and frailty.

. . .

So what is God, then—mother or father? Perhaps both. Or neither, because we are simply part of God. A spark that is cast off and returns to the original mass of light.

If this is true, then God has more than one ego.

. . .

Society today forgets that there are reasons why people and things have different roles in life. We make life more complicated by insisting that everything is equal.

· · ·

Certainties are short-lived in this world, though they may be obstinate and bear great changes that we will one day come to regret.

· · ·

In this world there exist languid moments and they are contagious. At such times, reason serves no more; it is best to give the brain a break and let yourself live.

· · ·

Sometimes there arise temporary cycles of atonement—talk of love and understanding—but then the system plows on, and that same talk is used to create new traps and complications for the fools who still think they're living in the previous cycle, the so-called love cycle.

. . .

That is what counts, always—as long as the evolution of life can never be taken seriously. Life? It's too silly, inexplicable and fickle. At a certain point you draw your conclusion, but we'll never know whether it's real or fake. One day our deck of cards will be reshuffled and then maybe we'll understand. For now, all we've got to do is live.

. . .

Bureaucracy exists, and it doesn't work very well. When you meet up with it in person, to survive you can approach it in either of two different ways. The first, and perhaps better, is to live out the experience with irony. It's like being at the circus watching the clowns perform—if they're really good, you split your sides laughing. The second is to reason things out calmly, trying to understand why certain obstacles have arisen. Insisting too much on the second method, however, is likely to drive you crazy.

. . .

Some people at the head of the system envision the expansion of bureaucracy as a healthy and necessary growth of the government as a corporation with an ever-increasing number of employees. Too bad these people missed one very important fact: A corporation of this type generates only costs and doesn't produce any wealth. Worse, the system places less importance on human ingenuity than on computer results, which are easy to control by just changing one factor.

. . .

Back in the old days, the powerful and the Mafia extorted people, whereas today the system does it legally. In one way or another, the people always end up paying. The methods used today are just more sophisticated.

. . .

Basically, the world has always worked this way. Generations of priests and preachers have lived by tricking the people and then providing solutions. They invented the Holy Inquisition, making use of an ingenious idea: "You must love and respect the Creator and act accordingly." Who could contradict a statement like that? It was right and good. What was not right and good were the aims and methods applied.

. . .

The more we demand an easy solution generated outside of ourselves, and the more we give power to committees and government, the more individuals of all colors and customs lose their very reasons for existing as individuals.

. . .

There will always be those who suffer, that's the way life has been designed. Let's not deceive ourselves so that we end up suffering even more, and get angry to boot, because we feel abandoned unto ourselves—some more, some less. There's just one basic rule to follow and it's this: The more fortunate ones must help the others, which, after all, is in their own best interests as well. You can't live a comfortable life with serenity if you're surrounded by sick, starving people willing to do anything just to survive.

. . .

I don't think we've ever gotten beyond the Stone Age. Just because we've discovered steel, uranium and computers doesn't change anything. We're still fighting over the same problem as our predecessors.

. . .

How different America was in the days of the founders of Ford, General Electric, Boeing and so forth. Those people needed capital for longterm plans, to run real factories with long-term balanced budgets and huge growth forecasts, where immediate earnings were often not the topmost priority. What happened? Buy, sell, buy, sell, mergers, buy-outs, etc....

. . .

The sensations and fixations of our time come and go quickly as if they had adapted to the rhythm of television, news and fashion.

Today, a decision is considered excellent and indispensable, tomorrow it is harshly criticized, after a week it is forgotten, and two months later, it is re-implemented.

. . .

Then, everyone's eyes are focused on that little group on the stage at the New York Stock Exchange on Wall Street, applauding and smiling brightly, thinking only one thing: Whatever happens, I've made some money. The incredible thing is that these people are convinced they've earned their money through hard work.

. . .

Most projects begin with big ideas fueled by enthusiasm, vision and creative inspiration. Those used to the process know how frequently creativity has to be muted to follow the boring requests of the market and the bureaucracy of the system in place. An idea born of brilliance can be watered down and become a mediocre reality. Dreams are put aside in the name of somber functionality; elegance forsaken to save a dollar. One day you find yourself facing that haunting question: "Will it still work?"

. . .

The trains go by, but if you don't show up at the station you cannot take one of them, not even the slowest.

. . .

How could an accountant and a salesman ever understand one another?

. . .

Unfortunately, humanity generally believes that the findings of scientists and scholars in general are precise judgments. Science says so. Wholly ignored are the doubts that assail researchers if they're honest. Every scientific discovery starts with a postulate, a statement, an act of faith. This is then elaborated on—and it is only at this point that rationality intervenes.

It is no coincidence that mathematical analysis may be defined as a "poetic science," where at times imagination has the upper hand over reality. Without mathematical analysis we'd still be making superficial observations of phenomena, and unable to interpret or extrapolate them....

The concept is easy to grasp—just read one of the many books written on Einstein. The problem is, however, that people do not wish to admit this. Everybody's either looking for a sure explanation for everything or giving you one, non-stop.... You can't explain everything, you have to submit to it. All you can do is interpret it and try to live together in a more constructive way.

. . .

In reality, we're the ones who no longer seek out the questions because we already know that only great faith in the existence of a word so often used and increasingly indefinable can buttress us. The word is Love…. What is Love? This is a question I continue to ask myself even if it always comes back to me more cloaked in mystery and loaded with contrasting decisions to be made than before. However, it is a question that must be further explored without hoping for a convincing answer. It's a question that requires lengthy research and intuition.

. . .

You never know which path
will bring you to serenity,
which is by nature temporary
but, like the flowers of the bougainvillea,
keeps re-emerging
covering the thorns.

THE CASTAWAY

The only thing that counts is love and the continuous search for it, whether through philosophy, art, poetry, sacrifice, faith or grace.

. . .

All too often, religion and laws do not agree with the message of love that is handed out in the name of God.

. . .

Religion should be a means to seek out love, understanding, sharing and forgiveness—a guide for improving respect and love for others, for oneself, for the world.

. . .

What does it matter whether Jesus was truly the son of God, or God himself, or just an exceptional man? We're all children of God, but Christ put forth the message of love, which is as relevant as ever, and which everyone can follow. Though in reality many believers and churches of all denominations seem to ignore it.

. . .

What do the words eternal and infinite mean? We use them in poetry, in sermons, in science, even in the most banal pop songs. In mathematics, two parallel lines are defined as two lines that meet only at infinity. Mathematics has even assigned a well-defined symbol to represent the concept of infinity. Is this symbol all we know about it?

. . .

If we try to tackle the concept of eternity, we feel lost. We get the shivers just trying to imagine it. Either that, or we abandon the idea, especially nowadays, when we're so used to considering minutes, even thousandths of seconds, as important features of our existence.

But whatever our attitude toward eternity, if we are honest with ourselves, we have to admit that it profoundly intrigues us. We can't imagine a timeless world, a world that isn't marked by sunrises and sunsets, though deep down inside we want to believe that eternity exists. Worse yet, when we mock it or deny it, we give it substance and make belief in its existence all the more real.

. . .

The problem is imagining it.

. . .

Even though man seeks freedom, he is unconsciously attracted by everything that looms above him and dominates him—whether it be tall mountains, church steeples, skyscrapers, religion, ideas and passions of all sorts—all of which actually circumscribe man's freedom to act.

. . .

We can cultivate our dreams and illusions, which are an important part of our existence, but they belong to us alone, and we are the only ones who may revel in them and cherish them. It is also up to us to control them so that they can be channeled, allowing us to escape, yet making a quick return to everyday reality when necessary.

. . .

You can't run away from life. You've got to pursue it with seriousness and serenity in order to get out of it as much as you can, and to soothe your ever-restless spirit.

. . .

Build your future, but take time out to nourish your spirit with what may seem useless non-utilitarian things, which are necessary for a complete, fulfilling life.

. . .

Money, when it comes down to it, has no flag, no boss, no fixed domicile. Money is extremely mobile—everyone is interested in it, everyone wants it, especially small-minded people that rail against it in the name of fairness and justice. Money follows well-drawn channels which, if managed with care and prudence, keep one safe from most major mishaps.

. . .

Growth. What does it mean? No one really ever understands it. It is supposed to be the future.

. . .

It is unfortunate that we don't learn at school how to develop the faculties that have been given to us at birth, along with the curiosity to discover and experience, and a sensitivity for understanding others. School helps us only to sharpen our technical skills, sometimes not even related to our talents.

. . .

It requires effort to seek out practicality in life and restore the proper measure of things, to rediscover a way of thinking and acting with simplicity. But it is possible by learning to apply two words which nowadays seem so antiquated, worn out, mocked and out of fashion: "common sense." In truth, common sense is something that people carry at the bottom of their souls. If they only stopped for a moment, listened to it, used it and spread it around.

. . .

Demons exist inside us, which we ourselves have created. They torment our existence and destroy any chance of delighting in the joy that may derive from the good experiences we have had, even if life carries with it an inevitable dose of disillusion and pain.

. . .

Faith and love for others and all that surrounds us are such simple sentiments. So much so that they don't create any waves or make the evening news, thus escaping the attention and interest of the rest of the world.

. . .

When events lose their color of novelty, they are forgotten and fade into the haze of everyday normalcy.

. . .

A mere sexual episode is intensely lived and consummated quickly. Genuine love is built through hard work and controlled enthusiasm over time.

. . .

While it may not be right to get carried away and pursue passion to excess, it is absurd to see "sin" in every sensual aspect of life, to fetter human beings' natural urges, thus making them easy prey to overindulgence once the dam holding back their passions crumbles.

. . .

Sexual desire can take hold with violence, then slowly relent; although it may return in mercurial spurts at first closer together, then farther apart, the ebb and flow like waves at sea when the stormy wind dies down.

. . .

Spiritual involvement, on the other hand, is solid and lasting. But if it cannot be put in perspective with the values of life, it can lead to debasement and dangerous delusions.

. . .

The sea is a mighty expanse of water;
its boundaries are the sky.

The sky is bounded by the universe,
and the universe is bounded by...

GOING BY SEA

Boats have always been better than their crews. All you have to do is keep them far from shoals, let them live in their element, water, and they'll always find a way to sail on in safety.

. . .

The roar of the sea is like a mirror that reflects your fears, your insecurities; but once you've heard it, it will return now and again to reinvigorate your spirit.

. . .

Nothing escapes the thoughts of human beings more than the conclusion of their own dreams— which is to say, the certainty of their very existence and their hopes for immortality.

. . .

It's like a punishment, sometimes sweet, sometimes bitter, that slows the unfolding of your present, but...you know you can always dream.

. . .

The invasion of pop-inspired communication in journalism and politics, where everyone has something to say and a deluge of talking heads pawn themselves off as experts and scientists, has by now reached the level of farce. The viewing audience is considered solely an entity to be manipulated, since people are thought to be incapable of figuring things out for themselves.

. . .

Unfortunately, in human beings anger often grows and leads them to seek blame and reasons that satisfy egos, so bombarded by politics, the media and religious fanaticism, without trying to grasp the full reality, which is sometimes much simpler that it appears.

That's how political parties come into being, and so, too, blind faith, myths, legends, along with the destruction of our search for the joy of life.

. . .

Emotion—another magic word that politicians, religious leaders and businessmen employ to enhance their power.

The abuse of emotions has evolved to such a degree of specialization—from religion to politics to "branding" in advertising—that is has taken on a life of its own, all in the name of progress.

Such progress controls emotion by instilling in the hearts and minds of human beings complex rules that create a mythology which offers certainty: So-called "sure" answers.

. . .

A minute is gone forever, and that minute has become our past. True, it still belongs to us. But what good is owning it? Who would ever steal the past in order to use it again?

After all, it is useless property.

A few years later it will resurface with other characteristics, assume a certain value and be called memory.

. . .

Memory—what is memory? Perhaps it is an insult to the future, like anxiety that grasps your soul?

We, however, must not fear, because whatever it may be, it belongs to us—it's almost impossible to have it stolen from us, but we can dissipate it.

. . .

In all likelihood, you'll die before your memory disappears.

. . .

The frenetic, obtuse greed of the financial system and its pursuit of quick profits have taken away any vestige of respect for the necessity to plan out the world's demands and ways of meeting them.

. . .

Bureaucracy, bordering on dictatorship, is capable of no more than enforcing—continually and to the letter—new rules that seem to have been thought up by people who would be of great interest to Sigmund Freud.

The sole result: destruction of this country's working spirit.

. . .

In today's world there is a lot of talk about freedom of speech, but at the same time, people in the name of political correctness control information, and we are increasingly exposed to politicized versions of the facts.

What is freedom of speech worth if we can only disperse it to the wind?

. . .

Shouldn't we be striving for that more meaningful freedom that allows us to live our lives with respect for the rules dictated by nature and human survival, the ones people still dare—secretly, behind closed doors—to call "common sense"?

. . .

Freedom, a concept often abused and misinterpreted, is more of a duty than a right—the duty to respect one's obligations and make a contribution to lessen society's problems and, possibly, seek to become an ambassador for the word "love."

. . .

It is true that we have been shaped by the violence of the natural world in which we live. When you watch in ecstasy the beauty of the sea or a serene landscape rife with greenery, you miss what is hidden beneath—the struggle for survival. To survive means to overpower others or to create alliances and build a safe platform from which it is easier to defend yourself.

. . .

All human knowledge, all the laws of physics, even the most precise, start from a premise, a postulate that is in practice an act of faith. We have learned to make those laws evolve, to develop them with mathematical precision and then use them to enrich our experiences, to simplify—or perhaps complicate— our lives. To sum it up in two words, to progress.

But what is that initial premise?

The only thing we can be certain of is that we have the ability to ask ourselves a variety of questions.

. . .

The world is overpopulated and people are voracious—they want too much. Here's an umbrella term for it all: mass stupidity.

JOURNEY
BEYOND 2012

Money's always part of the equation.

. . .

Wealth isn't necessarily a negative thing—on the contrary, it can be positive when used to help the world become more coherent by pursuing humanity's basic needs and simplifying life. But too often it is used to feed power and complicates everything.

. . .

Italy! It's a country that's tough to work in because of its absurd political system, and there's a crazy amount of bureaucracy. But the Italians, after the fall of Rome, over centuries became accustomed to living under various regimes, as well as under the rules laid down by ecclesiastical governance. That has taught them one important thing: to focus on making the best of life and not giving a hoot about all the rules. They always come up with a solution to any problem. When you observe them more closely, you notice that many of them feel like citizens of the world. You can find them everywhere, working, living, investing capital. But even if they criticize their own country, they always feel great nostalgia for it. The secret is to go to Italy on vacation, spend some money, but not get involved in their problems. If you take it like that, visiting Italy is really very pleasant. If you like, I can whip up a basic itinerary for you, that is, if you're interested.

. . .

In Italy, they have a saying about the many rules the government and its functionaries like to enforce: "It's like someone who places his penis on the table, decides to strike it with a hammer, and is overjoyed when he misses."

. . .

When your parents are no longer there to shelter and protect you, you realize that you're on the front lines now, alone and responsible for those following in your wake.... That was the reason why in the entrance to homes in ancient Rome there was a niche in the wall with statues of ancestors. People turned to their forebears for protection and comfort. They attempted to recreate that layer of parental protection in order to attain a feeling of temporary security.

. . .

After you've reached a certain age, the main goal is to find a place where you feel most comfortable. You seek serenity.

. . .

The world's population will continue to balloon because one race or religion wants to dominate all the rest. This competition will only lead to huge catastrophes that give the world a chance to survive and move forward with so-called new ideas. But when you look at history, they're actually ideas that have already been used, abused, rendered obsolete and abandoned. What do you think, that all this much-touted globalization is going to lead mankind to a world that is unified and functional?

. . .

People talk about globalization, but the bottom line is that everybody's waging their own finance wars, especially in the developing countries, not giving a damn about the conditions of average people, who are barely able to survive. They suffer, they curse their lot, but mostly they reproduce, exponentially. Then what happens? Disenfranchised, stripped of their own culture, intoxicated by what they see around them on television and the Internet, they become unruly, seek out new horizons, and migrate, creating further confusion.

· · ·

At first glance, the way people think about their place in the world proceeds along a slow, undulatory path, with long periods of almost imperceptible changes that at some point appear to gain speed and go to extremes, like a wave that has traveled for thousands of miles approaching land, finally cresting and crashing down on the beach... That is the way progress occurs in the world. Ideas always spring from those individuals who, when it comes down to it, are responsible for either progress or regression in the world.

. . .

The majority of people—and this goes especially for the politicians—think only of daily survival. And for them, ideas seem to be in hiding, as if in hibernation, but the ideas turn into reality in spite of them.

. . .

You have to live and live intensely. Perhaps one day, in an instant of space and time, or in something that is neither space nor time, we will find the answer to the question of our existence that has been lurking in our minds since the dawn of time.

. . .

Every profound change in human history has had adherents who welcomed it and detractors who resisted it with all their might.

. . .

Change comes slowly and never without pain.

. . .

Mankind is but a soup of bodies and spirits contorting and stirring themselves up, if only as an exercise to combat encroaching rheumatism and boredom.

. . .

The history of humanity is nothing but a slapping together of idiotic presumptions that pit everybody against everybody else in an ongoing quest for dominance through the conditioning of minds and the control of goods and services. It hasn't changed for thousands of years, and it never will!

. . .

The art of survival is in all of our DNA; it's been passed down to us for ages. When the time comes, you'll know exactly what to do.

. . .

Homo sapiens likes to talk, theorize, take on ideas and argue about such events. And then what? We go to sleep exhausted yet satisfied with the time spent chattering about the fate of the world, as if everything depended on the actions and will of human beings alone.

. . .

Human beings need to talk and talk some more, repeat themselves, and rack their brains to say the same things with slightly different nuances again and again.

. . .

If you say it in Latin, it must be true. Latin is a language that provides a sense of importance. You believe what it says!

. . .

Moral law is not always a precise abstract entity. It is perhaps influenced by years of intuition that form a culture which in some way remains fastened to the species known as *Homo sapiens*.

. . .

Day in and day out, mankind's reason has created laws, beliefs and a model of life that today are in crisis. And the crisis infuses each day with greater and greater urgency, as there seems to be less and less time to come up with a possible remedy. The speed of the electronic world, the growth of populations and their needs, the empty promises of governments, and the incapacity of humanity to embrace these pressing developments rationally has led us to create radical and fanciful solutions in response to our frustrations.

. . .

Surely everyone tries to employ different ways of thinking in order to improve and counter some of our predispositions, but the impulses that underlie and continue to influence and guide human minds are very strong, indeed.

. . .

Celestial bodies exert a certain influence not only on the tides, seasons and climate, but on humans as well.

If this is true for individuals, then why shouldn't the movement of the sun and its planets in relation to the zodiac have a certain influence on humanity as a whole?

. . .

Consider the feeling of helplessness you experience deep inside when you attempt to contemplate the concepts of eternity and infinity. First you wonder why you use those words, which define phenomena that are utterly incomprehensible to you. Whoever put them into your head anyway? My advice would be to stop thinking about them altogether, and you'll avoid tormenting yourselves. At our level everything is defined in terms of space and time.

. . .

Imagine, if you can, a dimension in which these two factors do not exist, and eternity and infinity—two concepts so mysterious for you today— will simply cease to be. They will no longer be necessary. If there's no time, then the word "eternity" is meaningless. If there's no space, then infinity cannot exist.

. . .

Science has only certain elements at its disposal to explain various phenomena and to use them to satisfy human needs, which may be either beneficial or lethal for mankind. There has always been profound disagreement among science, religion, poetry, rationalist thought, philosophy, intuition and so forth. But they're all just different sides of the same coin.

. . .

All these phenomena have their own spheres of action, and when your souls pass from one level to the next, you'll ask yourselves fewer and fewer questions and clear up many of your doubts. You will find that reason will be of less and less use to you as you follow your intuition the way a poet does when he writes a poem.

. . .

We who live on this Earth don't create anything, nor can we explain the origins of all this or the act of creation. The strange thing is that someone who believes in God is said to have faith, yet when someone claims to be atheist and believes there is no continuation of life beyond this planet, you fail to say that he, too, is following a faith, a credo. There are many postulates we consider true, which is to say, many matters of faith. Why?

. . .

People on Earth are always talking about God, going to heaven or hell, Judgment Day and so on. But the strength that lies within us will take care of all of that by itself, moving among the different levels and experiences.

. . .

It really doesn't matter who Christ was, we can leave that to the experts. What's important is the fact that the world was waiting for that message, and that the world adopted it and betrayed it. Oh, that message is still valid today, but it has been so misinterpreted and watered down that it has been drained of all its force.

. . .

Christ spread a simple message of love that is still alive in the world after two thousand years and continues to ply the consciences of many people with plenty of new questions. Christ did not found a new religion, but divulged a new vision of mutual understanding and accord. He referred to mankind as the children of God and considered everyone. He even foretold that we all could become like him.

. . .

Before Christ came along, there were others who had similar perceptions of love and forgiveness, but their ideas had not taken root in general consciousness.

. . .

The Christmas season is part of a sacred tradition that stretches back to well before the birth of Christ. This time of year has always been dedicated to ceremonies, celebrations and the exchange of gifts in many ancient civilizations. The Romans, around the time of the birth of Christ, called these holidays the Saturnalia, after Saturn, the god of agriculture and harvest time. The question is whether Christ chose to be born this time of year for these reasons, or whether the Christians made the two dates coincide in order to appropriate someone else's tradition and facilitate the spread of the teachings of Christ.

. . .

When Christ was alive, nature was an ominous phenomenon at best and provided a view of survival everyone adhered to: Defend yourself, dominate, kill or be killed, eat or be eaten. In the animal kingdom it is rare to find forms of collaboration. If there is a common theme or law, it is that of your own survival and the survival of your species; order and balance are achieved only thanks to a kind of ongoing war, which regulates the growth of populations and divides up power.

In the course of history, this law hasn't changed much, even if nowadays our consciences, at least as far as the Western world is concerned, have gained a new awareness that prizes working with and respecting others. There are biologists now who write about selfish genes and try to explain all of human behavior in terms of these natural laws."

. . .

Christ came to tell the world of a father we all have in common, and while this may be interpreted in a thousand different ways, it does point toward a road to redemption for our material existences. He talked in parables and provided only a vague explanation without going into much detail— perhaps he thought people were not yet ready for that. The question is: Are we ready for those details even today? Can we aspire to entry into a new era, one that will lead us to another level of existence?"

. . .

The notion of the apocalypse is deeply embedded in the human psyche, and in mythology and religious lore, from the Norse *Götterdämmerung* to the Book of Revelations in the New Testament. While this planet had certainly seen its share of enormous catastrophes in which entire species have been wiped out, life has continued regardless of what people have to say about it.

. . .

If we don't come up with an intelligent, peaceful solution—one that's acceptable to everyone and finds a system that regulates the survival of the species and the limiting of their proliferation in the world—then the only valid law is the one we've always known: living in a state of perpetual war in order to control and eliminate others that represent a danger to you and your family, and joining those who form a circle of protection around us as well.

. . .

The old civilizations, based on the divine right of kings, became intoxicated with Communism, fascism, and more recently, the deceptive power of consumerism. But none of them have satisfied the spiritual needs of humanity. Instead, they have exploded in an uncontainable, albeit vague, longing for freedom, without ever coming up with valid answers.

. . .

The word "freedom" has always been a protagonist in history's great upheavals. But did the changes that took place satisfy those who had enacted them as they chased after the myth of freedom? Perhaps freedom is not of this Earth, where too many factors and events affect the conditions of life, the flow of life, and it would forever remain a pipe dream. Even today we really do not know how to correctly define freedom, much less find it, enjoy it and maintain it. An almost absurd word—for if we're unable to find freedom, how are we ever going to hold onto it?

. . .

There have always existed factors unknown to us which influence the workings of the human mind. There may always be exceptions, but all they create are unhappy creatures, for whoever is aware of this flow and opposes it is doomed to feel like a voice screaming in the desert and must languish misunderstood in solitude.

. . .

We—all of humanity—must start over again and seek out simplicity.

. . .

Am I God?
There is no difference? I am always myself.

In reality, God and I, we have something in common:

We are two different forms, both difficult to understand in the totality of their being.

I am my own mystery, as God is a mystery for me.

ONE LIFE
MANY LIVES

Sleeping is an interesting activity. A state of se-mi-consciousness blends with the creativity of dre-ams.

. . .

Dreaming is living twice. Reconstructing a dream while awake is like trying to revive a past life, a recent past that belongs to us only in part. What's not really ours remains in the dream and has disappeared, perhaps in anticipation of another encounter.

• • •

One has to learn to perforate the skin and pulp to let the air of the world touch our innermost quarters. It is then that we feel the old and the young inside us blending. This process is not directly linked to our physical age, but to the number and type of experiences and disappointments we have lived through or carry within us in our genes or inherited from who knows what other lives.

. . .

A person may be old at twenty-five, and an older person may be ready to open up to a new life like a field of poppies in late spring.

· · ·

Tomorrow is like a pen stroke added to the line of your life. Tomorrow will be a consequence of your yesterday, a momentary summary of last week, last year. It will be further proof of the slow, inexorable changing of your life, which tends to repeat itself with practically unnoticeable variations. You do, however, fear facing the grand event—still unknown. It may be exciting, sad, boring, pulsing with tension, beautiful, even fatal in the most sinister sense of the word.

But "fatal" will just be an instant, then you'll be confronted by a fork in the road. Perhaps you won't be able to choose which direction to take, because the force that drives you will choose for you. Everything races on and the turn that makes sense for you will determine your new direction.

. . .

Dying alone in a hospital or car accident is accepted as normal.

Dying in a group is "pure terror." The humanity within us rebels. We have a job: to make sure our species survives. The job is hard and deeply rooted; it shakes us and often makes us act like heroes against our will.

. . .

Humanity keeps looking for peace but continues to flirt with the idea of war in different forms and shapes because it is bored.

In reality, we are a part of nature, which hides behind its beauty—a violent system that regulates the relationship between friends and enemies.

. . .

Who's in control? The wheel, the man on the seat, the weight of the bicycle and its rider, or the disconnected piece of road?

What matters is that the wheel keeps turning, the rider keeps pedaling, the large stones remain in their place, and the little ones are sent flying in all directions by the movement of the wheel.

. . .

It always takes a push or an inexplicable event to set anything into motion. The concept is so simple and clear for the scientific-minded, but it's tough to accept—it costs us our presumption of omnipotence.

. . .

We can discuss seemingly important things, seek out various kinds of company, get drunk, make love, sunbathe (using the necessary creams), go for a boat ride, swim, ski, travel, listen to music, root for our favorite sports team, and, and...

But the struggle remains, even if everything appears to move more slowly around us, as if the world were following our pace and satisfying our needs.

We may even delude ourselves into believing we have created our own, almost unassailable niche amid life's confusion.

Sorry, life hurries on.

. . .

We live to learn.

BRIDGE THROUGH THE STARS

It is fated…that life on Earth requires you to eat, wash, defecate, sleep, work, love, suffer, rejoice, argue…but above all, follow rules.

. . .

In the big city everyone does what he wants and shows others what he prefers them to see. In small villages there is little privacy; gossip can be terrible and no one can really escape it.

. . .

Humankind has not yet understood how to turn the material progress it has made into practical, positive actions, values and outcomes. Too many people are content to use its achievements to amass wealth, which in turn generates a host of parasites whose only purpose is to cheat and inflict violence on one another in order to ensure their own, minuscule personal gain.

. . .

In the banker's world money doesn't stimulate any creativity or dreams. It represents just numbers that indicate an amount, and they don't know what to do with it other than reinvest it to create more money.

. . .

The phenomenon of fundamental differences among people is an indisputable fact, despite the insistence of the so-called politically correct crowd that everyone is equal and alike, which has led to a foolish crusade to have them all adopt the same political and practical systems for the process of living.

Such crusades were one of the great nonsensical pursuits of the human race, whether it used guns and arrows or propaganda to spread religion, political programs, and philosophical theories and ideologies. These attempts to patch up inevitable problems created by human flaws for a short period of time were ultimately nothing but a pursuit of power. Humanity is very ignorant about its own nature, and its efforts to force everyone into a certain way of behaving only compound the problem.

Would it not be more interesting to acknowledge the differences among the planet's populations and find a common way to walk together respectfully, with the minimum amount of interference required to maintain the social order?

. . .

The media world is like a pond that is rather bo-ring to watch—merely reflections of the surroun-ding trees, some branches that have fallen in the water, birds that dive in, and fish that occasionally jump. But the fish that make a living there need more oxygen, so from time to time water rushes in, diverted from a nearby creek, and gets agitated as if heated to a boiling point, until the locks are closed again.

. . .

Live the moments for which we were created with sincerity and simplicity. It is a primordial law that does not recognize differences among species and sexes. But it should not be betrayed, abused, circumvented, forbidden or applied with violence.

. . .

A person is made up of brain, heart, flesh, blood and sex. To grow in every aspect of our being, we must embrace them all. Just like steam pressure operates a locomotive—its pistons, wheels, whistle and so on—we must keep the pressure alive to be vital!

. . .

Unions between people can have a variety of features, depths of feeling and different responsibilities. If one day your family grows in number, it will proportionally grow in the amount of involvement that generates a network of connections. You will build up a big pile of remembrances that hovers above your shoulders and those of the other family members. Your real commitment in life, if you're honest with yourself, is to always pursue and keep cherishing this hoard of memories that unites your family.

. . .

So many in today's society make the mistake of confusing love with an exchange of common and heightened sensations that are similar to what we experience with arts, sports, sexual experimentation, or even trading secrets and personal problems in a healing process for life's stresses.

. . .

People often misuse the phrase "to make love" thinking it only refers to sexual relations. But it encompasses so much more—jointly participating in an awareness of feelings, positive and negative, pleasant or sad, which can bring us joy, despair, ecstasy or melancholy.

. . .

Enjoying sex is a good exercise that brings us closer to our primordial time of creation and keeps relations alive between people. It serves other functions, too—procreation, making peace after an argument, exploring feelings of dominance and submission. There are many scenarios covered by the phrases "going to bed together" or "having sex,'" but they have nothing to do with making love. Love is something mysterious, a name we use to identify an incomprehensible flow, an influx of being that implants in the human mind the inexplicable thought we call "God."

. . .

Life is subject to a series of mortal dangers without a reliable, efficient program to protect its fragility and vulnerability.

• • •

Rationality constrains thought in narrow channels and imagination and fantasy, legacies of our divine origins, which provide a deeper perception and understanding. They know no boundaries or limits but must be nourished.

• • •

Consciousness and intelligence are mysterious for-
ces, even if a number of scientists are trying to find
some partial explanation for them since they seem
to be part of an unknown mechanism of the universe and occur everywhere, like stardust.

. . .

Does the soul have roots? Shouldn't it be floating in the force field that keeps life wandering in the universe, even if too many times we get a strong message that we belong to a particular place? We feel that we were born exclusively in this time, and we feel also a strong attachment to our parents and relatives...to such a point that we bury them not far away from us. Many people can't find peace if someone that they cherish dies far away or at sea where the body cannot be found.

. . .

There may be some truth to the theory that human beings love masochism. They always try to hurt themselves—better, kill themselves—because they have a vague intuition left in their souls that tells them things were better before, much better, but they can't remember why or how to replicate that status.

. . .

We are, all of us, wayfarers of the universe who don't yet understand why we travel on this Earth, where nature is fundamentally hostile to our presence. It may appear beautiful and serene on the surface, but when we look closer, the reality is crueler and more vicious—an intense battle for survival.

. . .

Can we escape and find a different world somewhere that does not follow the restrictions of space and time, or do we have to keep living inside this shell because nothing else exists outside our purview?

. . .

Contemplating stars is only a starting point that triggers some thoughts and questions: Why are we here? Why do we share space and time together with them? And, is it possible to sense something outside of our space-time continuum?

. . .

The darkness studded with stars remains as a concept unfathomable to us—infinity—and if our human mind is not capable of evolving toward new visions, new realities, all this will be for us just like a big ocean without shores, lacking any use for us; and we will lose the awareness to have been ourselves and have been part of humanity.

. . .

The dark matter where the energy of the universe is hiding exists everywhere and perhaps forever.

Perhaps when our dreams or souls reach its interior, we will become an integral part of it and of the concept of eternity and infinity because we are made of the same stuff. Everyone thinks that the force which propels the cosmos, which many people call God, is outside the physical universe, but in reality, it could be the dark matter and we are tiny, experimental slivers that belong to it and will return to it.

· · ·

Among the myriad galaxies and other planets in the universe, the likelihood of generating intelligent life may be quite small. It happened on Earth. At the beginning, the development progressed very slowly until, at a certain moment, there was an almost inexplicable acceleration of understanding and consciousness that produced a rapid evolution of human knowledge. This phenomenon tends to reoccur after long periods of stasis, which feels like a kind of hibernation. We are experiencing such a leap now and we wonder, almost frightened, what causes it and where it comes from.

. . .

Discovery is a drug that raises man up to God, and curiosity is the first symptom of this process.

. . .

Encouraging the desire to know is not a selfish act.

. . .

The notion of eternity and infinity is such a deep-rooted thought or even obsession in itself, that it must be a reality.

. . .

I run toward infinity even though it will take me an eternity to find it.

. . .

Acknowledgments

I want to give special recognition to my dear friend, Richard Storm, with whom I spent many hours discussing music, the arts and other wonderful things of the world. He encouraged me to put together this little book of quotes and enjoyed an early draft that I shared with him. But he left us for greater horizons before it was published.

A big thank you goes to **Vanessa Houston** from the bottom of my heart for her generosity. I never release a book in English without her blessing.

. . .

Piero Rivolta

was born in Milan, Italy in 1941 and practically grew up in the automobile and motorcycle factory that created the famous Isetta "bubble" car, luxury IsoRivolta sports cars, and the Formula One Team IsoRivolta Marlboro. After running the company from the middle 1960s to the early 1970s, he embarked on many other business ventures around the world while still designing cars, including breeding jumping horses, but he always pursued his love of writing. In 1979, after having endured 10 years of stifling government socialism in Italy, he left his beloved birthplace only for one reason—to explore a country where creative freedom of action and thinking held much promise: the United States of America. Since then he has engaged in a variety of ventures, including real estate development and luxury boat building because of his passion for ocean sailing, hoping that this quality will endure. In this context, Piero has written and published five novels, *The Castaway, Sunset in Sarasota, Beyond 2012, Bridge Through the Stars and Alex and the Color of the Wind. His volumes of poetry include Nothing Is Without Future; Going By Sea; One Life, Many Lives and Just One Scent: The Rest Is God.*

Made in the USA
Las Vegas, NV
08 February 2022

43396408R00115